THE BUSHCRAFT HANDBOOKS

KNOTS & LASHINGS

Illustrations by the Author

Richard H. Graves

The Bushcraft Handbooks
Knots & Lashings

This Edition Copyright © 2013 by Palmer River Publishing

Cover, Graphics and Layout by: Palmer River Publishing

ISBN-13: 978-1484820780
ISBN-10: 1484820789

About The Author

The author of "The Bushcraft Handbooks", Richard Graves, is a member of the Irish literary family of that name.

A veteran of the Great War campaigns in the Dardenelles and the Western Front, the author became passionate about the bush at an early age. As an enthusiastic bushwalker, skier and pioneer of white-water canoeing, he foresaw how a knowledge of bushcraft could save lives in the Second World War. To achieve this end, he initiated and led the Australian Jungle Rescue Detachment, assigned to the Far East American Air Force. This detachment of 60 specially selected A.I.F. soldiers successfully effected more than 300 rescue missions, most of which were in enemy-held territory in New Guinea, without failure of a mission or loss of a man.

An essential preliminary for rescue was survival, and it was for this purpose that the notes for these books were written. These notes were later revised and prepared for a School in Bushcraft which has been operating for several years and continues to provide valuable instruction to Servicemen embarking overseas on active service in Korea and Malaya.

Bushcraft

As far as is known, "The Bushcraft Handbooks" are unique. There is nothing quite like them, nor is any collection of published bushcraft knowledge as comprehensive.

The term "Bushcraft" is used because "woodcraft" commonly means either knowledge of local fauna and flora or else is associated with the blood-sports of hunting and shooting. "The Bushcraft Handbooks" include a volume on traps and snares, but these are purposely-designed to be completely ineffective for native animals which are insect enters or grazers. These traps have been included because they would only be effective in catching predatory animals such as cats and dogs which have taken to the bush, and other "pest" creatures such as feral swine or goat.

"Bushcraft" describes the activity of how to make use of natural materials found locally in any area. It includes many of the skills used by primitive man, and to these are added "white man" skills necessary for survival, such as time and direction, and the provision of modern "white man" comforts as illustrated in the volume on bush campcraft.

The practice of bushcraft develops in an individual a remarkable ability to adapt quickly to a changing environment. Because this is so, the activity is a valuable counter to the over-specialisation so prevalent in today's society, and is particularly significant in youth training and character-moulding work.

INTRODUCTION to the BUSHCRAFT HANDBOOKS

THE PRACTICE OF BUSHCRAFT shows many unexpected results. The five senses are sharpened, and consequently the joy of being alive is greater.

The individual's ability to adapt and improvise is developed to a remarkable degree. This in turn leads to increased self-confidence.

Self-confidence, and the ability to adapt to a changing environment and to overcome difficulties, is followed by a rapid improvement in the individual's daily work. This in turn leads to advancement and promotion.

Bushcraft, by developing adaptability, provides a broadening influence, a necessary counter to offset the narrowing influence of modern specialisation.

For this work of bushcraft all that is needed is a sharp cutting implement: knife, axe or machete. The last is the most useful. For the work, dead materials are most suitable. The practice of bushcraft conserves, and does not destroy, wild life.

R.H.G.
April, 1952

CONTENTS

KNOTS & LASHINGS

The ability to join two pieces of natural material together, and so increase their length, gives man the ability to make full use of many natural materials found locally.

Sailors probably did more to develop order in the tying of knots, because for them it was necessary not only to tie securely but also to be able to untie, often in the dark and under conditions of bad weather and with rain-tightened ropes.

In bushcraft work probably half a dozen knots would suffice, but knots and knotting have a fascination for many people the world over, and a comprehensive range of knots, plain and fancy, and, with these, splices, whipping, plaits, and net making are included in this book with information of general use.

Knot tying is a useful exercise to obtain better coordination between eyes and fingers. The identification of knots by feel is an excellent means of developing recognition through touch.

In all woodcraft work it is necessary to know how to tie knots which will hold securely and yet can be untied easily. Many of the materials which you will have to use will be green, some will be slippery with sap, and there are many little tricks and knacks to get the best possible use from the materials available.

Knots and lashings take the place of nails for much

bushwork, and when it comes to traps and snares, a thorough knowledge of all running knots is essential.

A brief description of the use to which the knot may be put is given in this book. The diagrams will explain how the knot is tied. The letter "F" means the free or untied end of the rope, and the letter "S" means the standing or secured end.

Knots for Rope Ends of for Grips on Thin Rope

THUMB KNOT
To make a stop on a rope end, to prevent the end from fraying or to stop the rope slipping through a sheave, etc.

OVERHAND KNOT
Overhand knot may be put to the same use as the thumb knot. It makes a better grip knot, and is easy to undo.

FIGURE EIGHT
This knot is used as the thumb knot. Is easy to undo, and more ornamental.

Knots for Joining Ropes

SHEET BEND
To join or bend two ropes of unequal thickness together. The thicker rope is the bend.

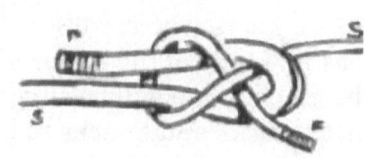

DOUBLE SHEET BEND

Similar to single sheet bend, but gives greater security, also useful for joining wet ropes.

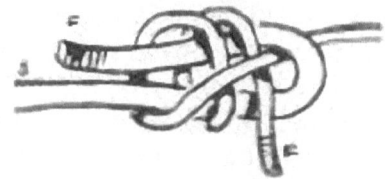

CROSSOVER SHEET BEND

This holds more securely than either the single or double sheet bend and has occasional real uses such as fastening the eye of a flag to its halyard where the flapping might undo the double sheet bend.

REEF KNOT

To securely join two ropes of equal thickness together. Notice the difference in position of the free and standing ends between this and the thief knot.

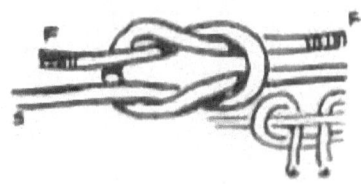

THIEF KNOT

To tie two ropes of equal thickness together so that they will appear to be tied with a reef knot, and will be retied with a true reef knot. This knot was often used by sailors to tie their sea chests, hence the name.

CARRICK BEND

This bend is for the secure fastening of two ropes of even thickness together. It is particularly suitable for hawsers and steel cables. It can be readily undone and does not jam, as do many other bends and knots.

STOPPER HITCH

To fasten a rope to another rope (or to a spar) on which there is already a strain. When the hitch is pulled tight the attached rope will not slip, and the tension on the main rope can be taken on the attached rope. Also useful for a climbing hitch.

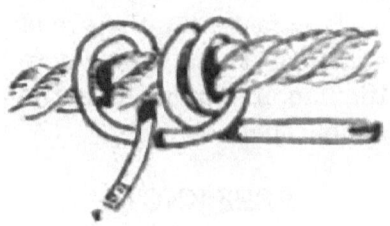

FLEMISH KNOT or DOUBLE OVERHAND KNOT

For securing two ropes or cords of equal thickness together.

FISHERMAN'S KNOT

For joining two springy materials together; suitable for wire, fishing gut or vines. Two thumb knots (one on each rope) pulled tight. The knots lock together.

OVERHAND FISHERMAN'S KNOT

Similar to fisherman's knot; for general uses. More positive for gut fishing lines and nylon.

Knots to Make Loops in Rope

BOWLINE

To form a loop that will not slip on a rope end.

BOWLINE ON A BIGHT

To make a double loop that will not slip on a rope end. Also called a bo'sun's chair.

FISHERMAN'S EYE KNOT

This is the best method of making a loop or eye in a fishing line. The strain is divided equally between the two knots.

SLIP KNOT

For fastening a line to a pier or a pole or any other purpose where strain alone on the standing end is sufficient to hold the knot.

OVERHAND EYE KNOT

This method of making an eye or loop is satisfactory and quick, but it sometimes jams and becomes difficult to untie.

FLEMISH EYE KNOT

Used for all purposes, where a loop is required, less likely to jam than overhand eye knot.

CRABBINS HITCH

This eye knot, though not very well known, is one of the stoutest eye knots. It has not the tendency to cut itself or pull out common to some of the other eye knots. It also makes a useful running knot.

MANHARNESS KNOT

This is a most useful knot for making a series of non-slip loops in a rope for the purpose of harnessing men for a pull. The marlinspike hitch is made as in lower sketch and then the loop is drawn under and over the other two ropes as indicated. The whole knot is then pulled taut.

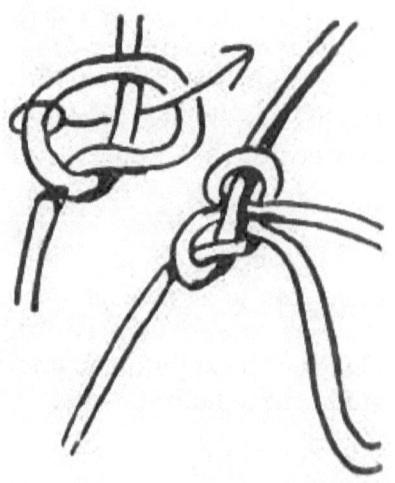

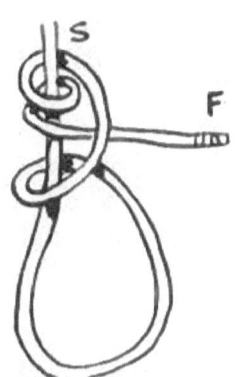

MIDSHIPMAN'S HITCH

This is an old-fashioned hitch often used to fasten a block or sheave to a rope's end.

JURY KNOT or TRUE LOVER'S KNOT

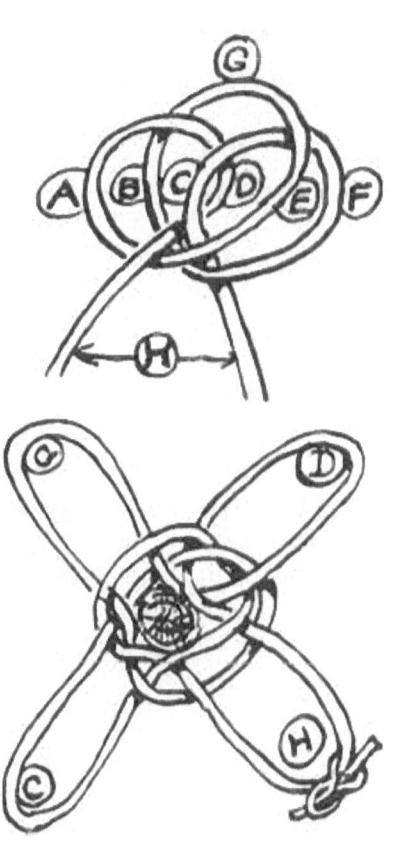

This knot is primarily for a mast head, to form loops by means of which the mast may be stayed. It is called a jury knot because in sailing ship days it was often used to rig a temporary or jury mast.

Three hitches as in top sketch are formed. The loop C is pulled under B and over A. D is pulled over E and under F. G is pulled straight up for the third loop. H is made by splicing the two free ends together.

BOW THONG HITCH

Used by New Guinea natives for securing the end of the split cane bow thong to the pointed end of the bow. Also useful for fastening rope over the tapered end of a spar.

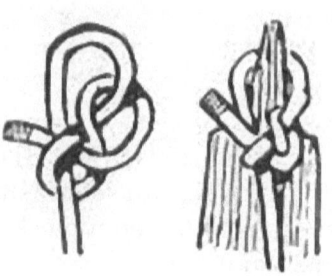

Knots for Fastening Ropes

SLIPPERY HITCH

Very useful because of the ease with which it can be released in emergency. It holds securely for so long as there is a strain on the standing end.

CLOVE HITCH

For securing a rope to a spar. This hitch, if pulled taut, will not slip up or down on a smooth surface. A useful start for lashings.

BOAT KNOT

This is a method of securing a rope to a thole pin or other small piece of wood on a boat. It is quickly released.

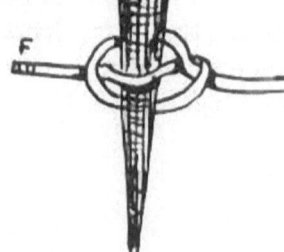

DOUBLE BOAT KNOT

A bight is simply passed through the ring and a marlin spike or other round piece of wood is put between the bight or the rope. Withdrawal of the spike quickly releases the knot.

SLIPPERY HITCH

Very useful because of the ease with which it can be released in emergency. It holds securely so long as there is a strain on the standing end.

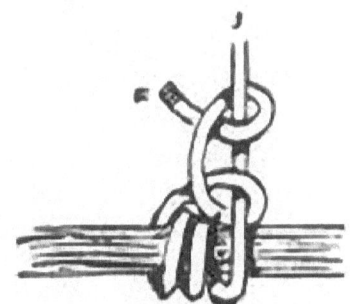

ROLLING HITCH

To fasten a rope to a spar. This is a very secure fastening.

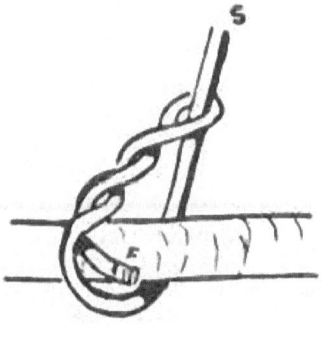

TIMBER HITCH

For securing a rope to squared timber, round logs, etc. A good starting knot for all lashings. The standing end must pull straight through the loop, not backwards, or the rope may cut upon itself.

HALLIARD HITCH

For fastening a rope to a spar. The sketch shows the hitch open. When pulled taut, and the hitches closed, it makes a very neat and secure fastening.

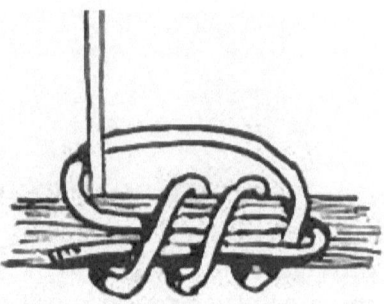

BLACKWALL HITCH

A quick way to secure a rope to a hook. The strain on the standing end will hold the rope secure to the hook.

NOOSE HITCH

This is a quick and easy method of securing a rope to a spar or beam. If desired, the rope can be made more secure by means of the overhand knot shown in Fig. 2.

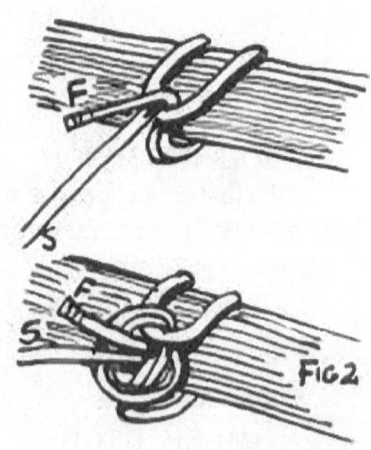

CAT'S PAW HITCH

For securing a rope to a hook or a spar. It is most useful because it is so easily tied.

LARK'S HEAD

This is an easy method of securing a rope to a ring or hook. If desired to make more secure, it can be stoppered, as shown, with an overhand or thumb knot.

CROSSOVER LARK'S HEAD

Used for purposes above.

DOUBLE LARK'S HEAD

The bight is first made. The ends passed through it. This knot is very secure.

TRIPLE LARK'S HEAD

The apparently complicated knot is easily made by taking the bight of the rope through the ring, the ends are passed through the bight and up through the ring, then down through its own bight. Like the double lark's head, this knot is absolutely secure.

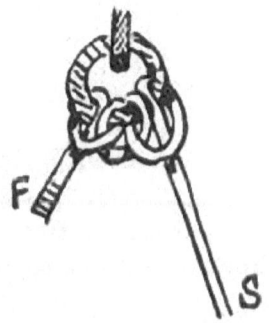

SAILOR'S BACKHAND KNOT
Used to secure a rope to a ring or hook. This is very similar to the Rolling Hitch (page 9) and Sailor's Backhand Knot (alternative variation) shown below.

SAILOR'S KNOT
Simply two half hitches round the standing end of the rope.

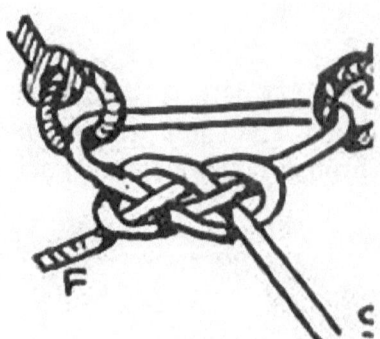

GUNNER'S KNOT
This is simply a carrick bend and used to hold two shackles or rings together.

SAILOR'S BACKHAND KNOT
(Alternative variation.) Used to fasten a rope securely to a spar.

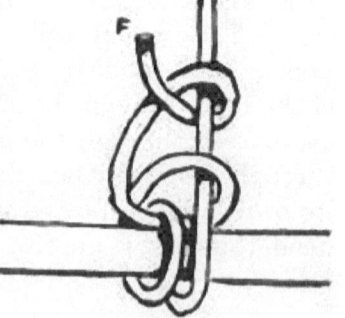

CATSPAW

This knot is used for attaching a rope to a hook. The two bights are rolled two or three times and then put over the hook.

KELLICK HITCH

Used for fastening a stone (for a kellick in lieu of an anchor), that will hold in rocky sea bottoms where an anchor might foul. It is a timber hitch finished off with a half hitch.

TOM FOOL'S KNOT

Formed by making a clove hitch as two loops not exactly overlaying each other. The inner half of each hitch or loop is pulled under and through the outer side of the opposite loop, as indicated by arrows.

This knot can be used to improvise a handle for a pitcher by pulling the centre knot tight around the lip of the pitcher and using the loops as handles.

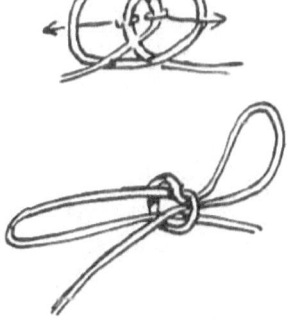

SHEEPSHANK
This is a convenient knot to quickly shorten a rope.

One method of securing the end.

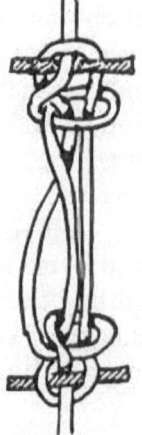

SHEEPSHANK TOGGLED
The insertion of a toggle in the end secures the sheepshank against slipping.

DRUM SLING
A slip knot is made as indicated. The drum, can or barrel is placed in the slip knot and the free end is secured with a stopper hitch to the standing end.

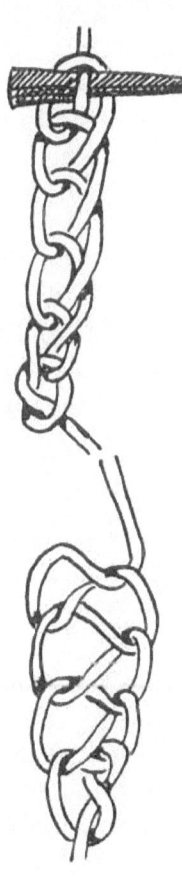

CHAIN KNOT
When a rope is too long for its purpose one means of shortening it is the chain knot. Remember to put a marlinspike or toggle through the last link before you put a strain on the rope.

DOUBLE CHAIN KNOT
This is the most ornamental of all the rope shortenings. A turn is taken round the standing end and the free end is passed through the loop so formed. In doing this a loop is formed through which the free end is brought. The end is thus passed from one side to the other through the loop preceding. It may be pulled taut when sufficiently shortened and will lock upon the last loop.

TWIST KNOT

This is another easy method of shortening a rope. The rope is laid as in Fig. 1 and then the strands are plaited or braided together. A marlinspike or toggle is placed between the ropes in the centre to secure the hold of the plait.

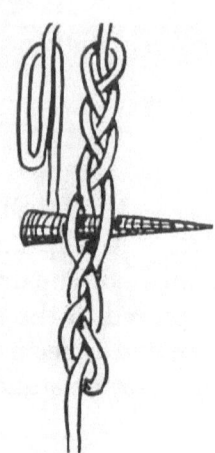

Fancy Knots

WALL KNOT

Unlay the rope a few inches and then pass each strand through the bight of the strand in front. Illustration shows the wall knot ready to be pulled taut.

STOPPER KNOT

Bring the ends of the wall knot round again and up in the centre of the knot and pull each one taut separately.

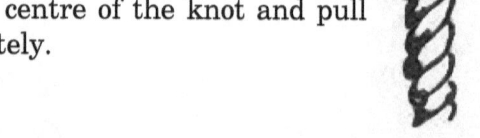

CROWNING KNOT

Commence the crowning as shown here.

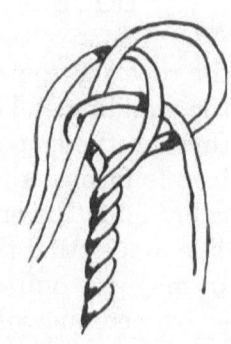

The crowning is now ready to be pulled taut. The strands can be back spliced to permanently secure the end of the rope against ravelling or fraying. Crowning may also be used with other fancy knots such as

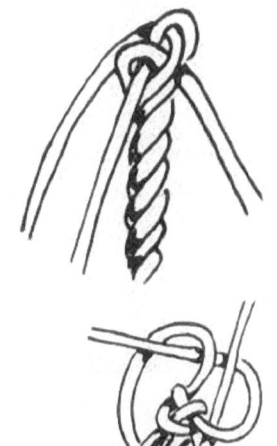

crowning first, then pulling on a wall knot or a Mathew Walker.

MANROPE KNOT

This is a fancy knot to put a stop on the end of a rope. Top sketch shows the crowning (in the centre), and lower sketch shows the man-rope knot pulled taut.

DOUBLE-DOUBLE CROWNING KNOT

This knot is started the same as the manrope, but not pulled taut. The ends are laid for a second crown above the crown (similar to the manrope knot) and with the spike the bends of the lower crown are opened, and the strands brought through these bends and pulled taut.

MATHEW WALKER 1

The strands are laid as in the diagram and then each in turn is pulled taut till the knot is close and tight. The knot itself is rolled up slightly to lay the twist evenly. Pull the strands tight again after this.

MATHEW WALKER 2.
Finished and rolled tight.

The Mathew Walker is reputed to be one of the most difficult of all knots to undo. The Mathew Walker can also be made some distance from the end of the rope and the strands then relaid.

DIAMOND KNOT

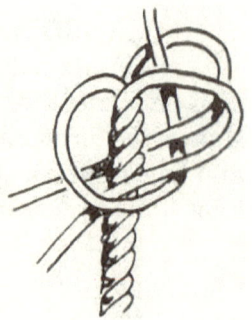

Like the Mathew Walker, the diamond knot is ornamental–can be made same distance along the rope. The rope is unlaid carefully. Each strand is brought down alongside the standing end, as illustrated (top). The strands are then put through the loops formed by the other strands in lower sketch. The strands are hauled taut. The rope relaid. Shows the finished diamond knot.

DOUBLE DIAMOND KNOT

This is made as for the single diamond knot, but the strands follow the lead of the single knot through two single loops. The last strand comes through two double loops. The strands come out through the centre when the knot is pulled taut. All these stopper knots can be used for the ends of lanyards, halyards, yoke lines and also as stoppers on cleats, and for rope buckets.

TURK'S HEAD

This is a highly ornamental knot which, instead of being made with the rope strands of the rope itself, is formed with smaller cordage on the rope.

A clovehitch is made as in Fig. 1. This is made slackly to allow the extra strands to be worked through it. Pull the bottom part of the hitch above the top part and put the free end under and up (Fig. 2). The now bottom strand is pulled above the top part and the free end now over and down. This repeat till the circle is complete. The free end follows round three times. The completed Turk's head is shown in Fig. 3.

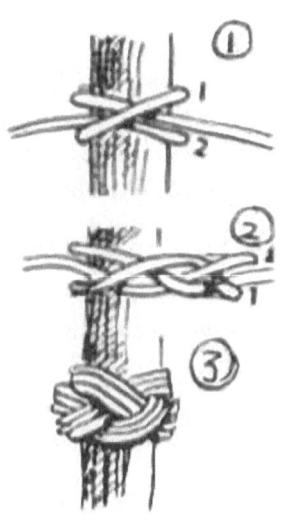

SHAMROCK KNOT

This may be formed the same way as the true lover's knot, but the bottom loop is not spliced. It may also be used to form three loops for stays for a mast. It may also be formed by making a knot as top sketch. The loop C is drawn up through loop D and the loop B is drawn up through the loop at A. These form the side loops and the top loop is formed naturally at E.

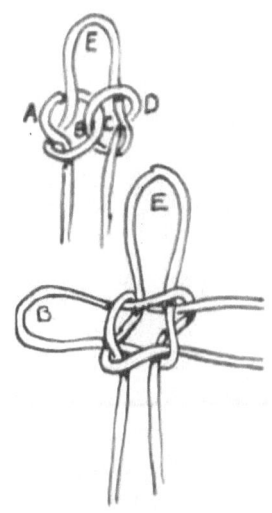

BUTTON KNOT

Form two crossover hitches, as Fig. 1. Pass the loop end to the left and with the free end form another loop as shown. Now, with the free end, follow the lay as indicated in Fig 2 and lay the strands side by side as for the Turk's head. When three to five lays have been put through, work the knot tight and use the free ends to fasten the button to the garment. A bootlace makes an excellent button.

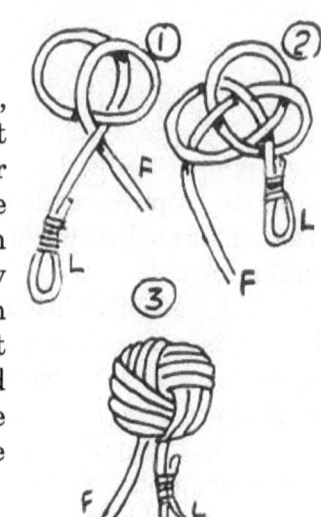

SELVEDGE

To secure a block to a standing spar. The middle of the selvedge is laid on the spar and the two ends are crossed over in turns until the bights at the ends come together. The hook of the block is then put through these two bights.

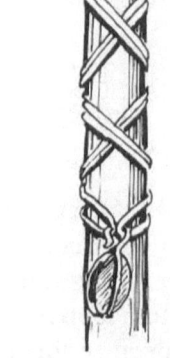

POINTING A ROPE

The rope is unlaid and a tie put on to prevent it unlaying further. The strands are thinned down gradually, and relaid again. The end may be stiffened with a small stick or piece of wire. The end can be finished off with any of the crown or wall knots.

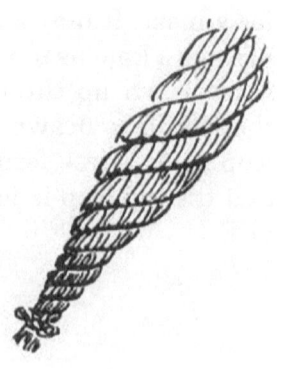

KNOTTED ROPE LADDER

The length of rope is coiled in a series of half-hitches and the end of the rope is passed through the centre, as in illustration on right (except that the coils are held close together as for a coiled rope when it is to be thrown). The coil of half-hitches with the end passed through the centre is turned inside out, that is, the succeeding coils are pulled over each other. The coil is now thrown, and as it pays out a series of overhand knots are made at fairly equal intervals. In making a knot ladder this is the quickest and most efficient method

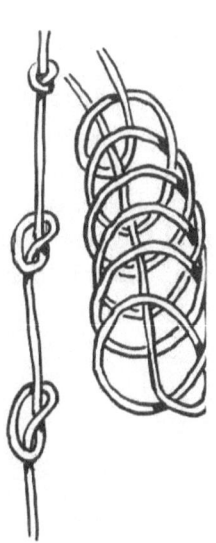

SINGLE ROPE LADDER
WITH CHOCKS

This type of ladder has the advantage of being portable and quickly made. The chocks of hardwood are about 6" diameter and 2" deep, and are suitably bored to take the diameter of the rope. Splice an eye at the top end and seize in a thimble to lash the rope head securely. To secure the chocks, put two strands of seizing between the strands of the rope and then work a wall knot.

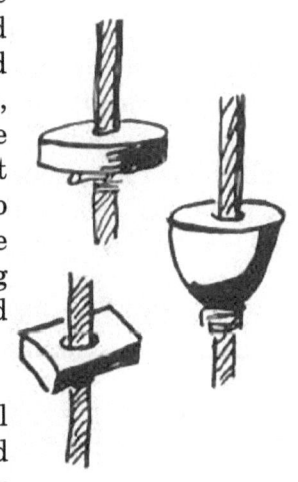

Alternatively, insert small pegs between the rope strands, and seize the rope with a binding below the pegs.

Lashing

SQUARE LASHING to join poles at right angles.

Start with a timber hitch or a clove hitch below cross bar. If using a timber hitch see that the pull is straight through the eye and not back from it. Pulling back will cut the lashing material.

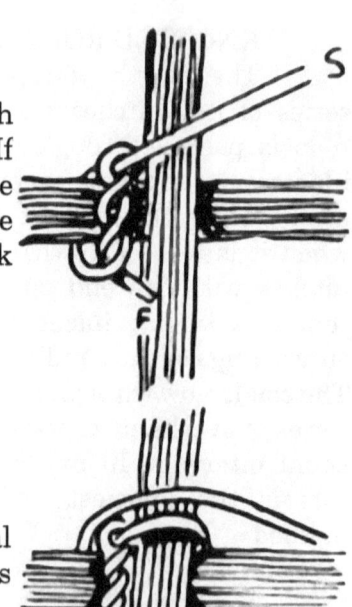

Put lashing material tightly around upright and cross bar about four complete times.

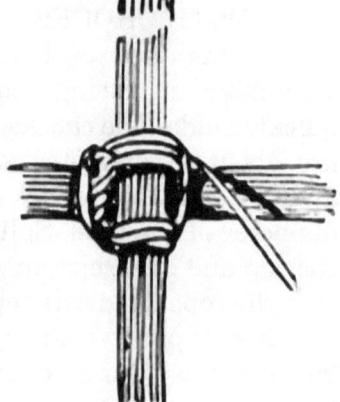

Frapping turns.—Make about two or three frapping turns. These are turns that go round the lashing and pull it taut. These pull the lashing tight. Secure end of frapping turns either by half-hitches or by passing between lashing at the crossover and secure with a half-hitch.

DIAGONAL LASHING for bracing or joining spars at irregular angles.

Start with a timber hitch or a clove hitch and take about three or four full turns vertically.

Pass rope under top spar and make about three of four full turns horizontally.

Make two or three trapping turns and either secure by two half-hitches on pole or by passing the end between the lashing and the pole and use halt-hitches, on the lashing.

SHEER LASHING to join two poles end to end.

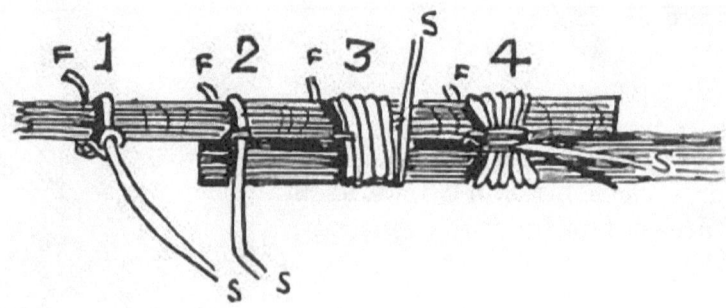

Start with a clove hitch or timber hitch, lash as in 1 and 2 tightly around the two spars four to six times as in 3. Pass free end under lashings and draw tightly two or three times. Secure by passing it through itself, as in 4.

There should be at least two lashings if spars are being joined together.

Splices

SHORT SPLICING

Unlay the strands and marry them together; butt hard up to each other. The strand D first goes under the standing end of A, but over strand B and over C on the standing end. Thus each strand at either end goes over one strand of the standing end on the opposite side and under the next strand, so that there is a strand of the standing end between each short side of the splice. Continue working the free strand of each end four or five times into the strands of the standing end.

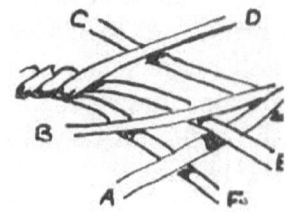

LONG SPLICING

The strands are unlaid for a considerable length and then married as for the short splice. Then the one strand is unlaid and its married counterpart is laid along its place in the rope.

The two centres are simply held with a crossover knot, and the strands thinned down and spliced as for a short splice. The end strands are finished with a crossover knot and again the strands are thinned down and finished as for a short splice. This long splice does not appreciably thicken a rope which may be thus spliced to go through a sheave.

LOOP SPLICE WITHOUT A FREE END

The rope is untwisted to the required place, as in top illustration. The free ends so formed are then spliced back along the rope after the loop has been formed.

EYE SPLICE

A neat eye can be made in a rope end by an ordinary short splice after the loop or eye has been formed.

WHIPPING

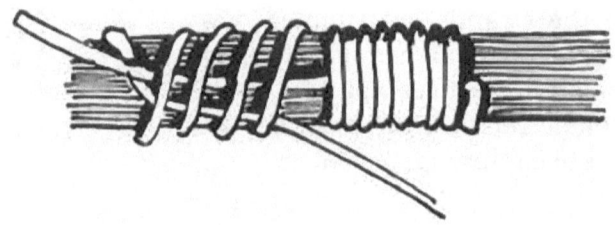

This is another method. After pulling taut, the two free ends are cut close in and the whole binding is smooth and neat.

LOOP SPLICE

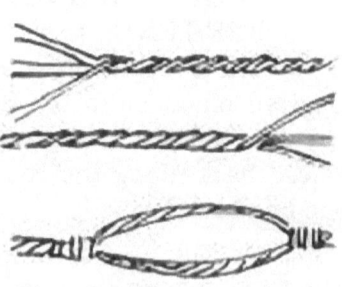

The strands are unlaid and laid side by side till the loop is the required length. The strands of the free ends are spliced into the ropes of the standing ends as for a short splice.

Toggle and eye–showing one application of splicing and whipping. Toggle is spliced and eye is whipped in sketch.

Binding or Whipping

WHIPPING

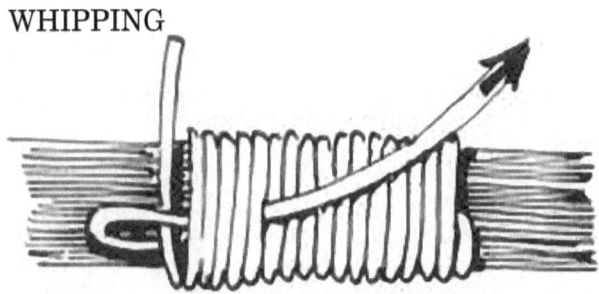

Before the finish of the binding a loop formed from the end is laid under the binding at the start. This end is bent back to form a loop and the last six to twelve turns bind over this loop. At the last turn of the binding the cord is put through the loop and the free end of the loop is pulled tightly, thus drawing the end of the binding beneath the last turn.

Netting

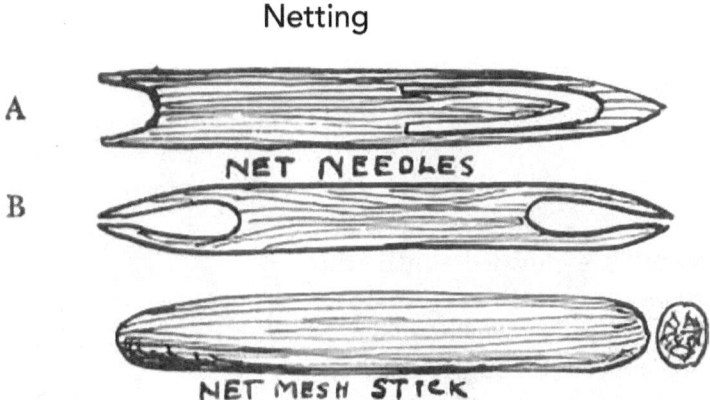

A

B

NET NEEDLES

NET MESH STICK

Hammocks and nets are made by the use of a netting needle and a mesh stick. Either of the two types of netting needle shown in Fig. 1 are suitable and easily made from a thin piece of hardwood or bamboo. The netting needles may be about 8 to 9 inches long and from f inch to 1 inch wide. The mesh stick may be about 5 inches long, oval about ¾ x ¼. The netting cord is put on to the netting needles as for an ordinary shuttle with needle B, and with needle A the cord is looped round the pin in the centre of the eye.

At one end of the string tie a loop and place the knot on a conveniently high nail or hook. The mesh stick is put under the loop and the needle with cord passed through as in Fig. 3. The needle and cord are passed in front of the loop formed in Fig. 3 and under the original loop, while at the same time the other end of the cord is held on to the mesh stick with the thumb of the left hand. The knot is pulled taut.

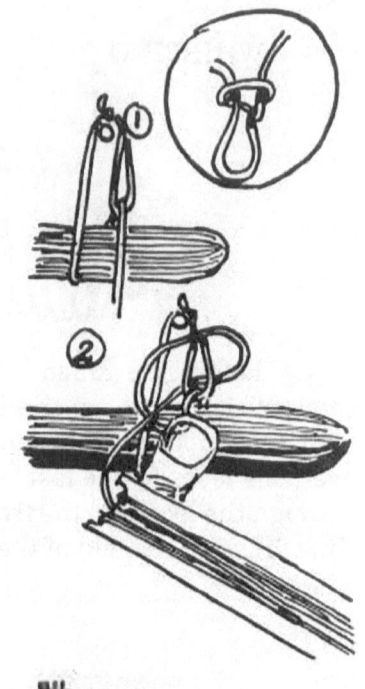

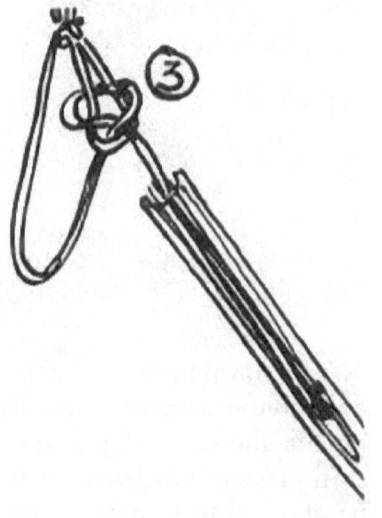

A succession of these loops are formed until the requisite width is reached, then this first series of loops are placed through a rod or cord, and the loops are netted on to them until the requisite length is reached.

Other Rope Techniques

ANCHORING A PEG IN SAND OR SNOW

The only way to anchor a rope into soft sand is to attach it to a peg, and bury the peg in the sand.

Scrape a trench in the sand to a depth of between a foot and eighteen inches, deeper if high winds or very stormy weather are expected. Pass the rope round the centre of the peg; scratch a channel for it at right angles to the peg trench.

Fill in the trench and rope channel, and fasten the free end of the rope to the standing end with a stopper hitch, and pull taut. The buried peg should hold a tent rope in sand under all normal weather conditions.

TO ANCHOR A ROPE IN OPEN GROUND

A secure anchor in open ground can be obtained by driving a stout stake well into the ground. The rope is later fastened to the base of this stake.

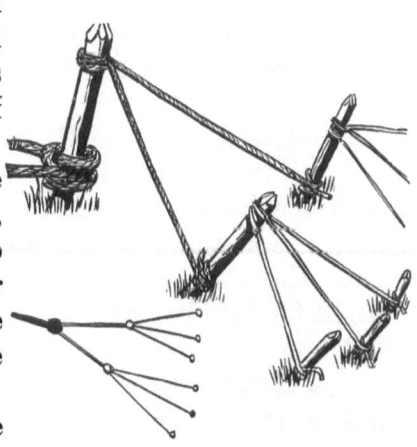

To the head of the stake two ropes are attached, and these are tied back to the ground level of two other stakes driven well into the earth a few yards behind the first stake.

To the heads of these

two stakes three ropes are tied and these are fanned out and tied to the bases of three other stakes driven in behind the two stakes.

The main rope is now fastened to the base of the first stake.

This is appropriately called the "ONE - TWO - THREE" anchor and will hold a very great strain if the ground is "solid."

BUSH WINDLASS

A bush windlass, capable of taking a very heavy strain on a rope can be made by selecting a site where a tree forks low to the ground, with the fork facing the direction in which the pull is required. Alternatively, a stout fork can be driven in and anchored with the "1-2-3" method.

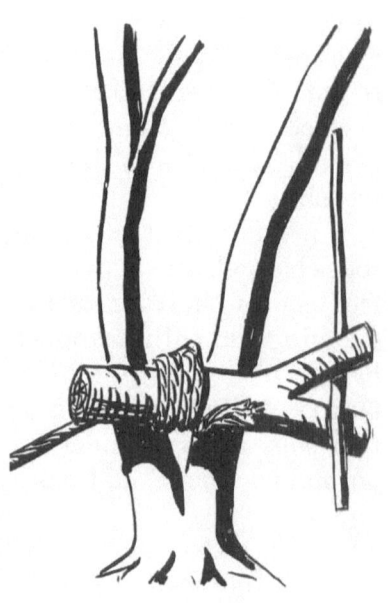

The windlass portion is a forked log. The forks are notched to take the lever (up to seven feet long). The rope is passed round the roller a few times so that it locks upon itself. (If the fork of the roller is long, the rope may pass through the fork.)

This type of bush windlass has many uses.

LARIAT OR ROUND PLAIT

1. Strand 4 is taken and passed over strands 2 and 3, and then turned behind the strand 2 and brought forward between 2 and 3.

2. Strand 1 (on the opposite side) is taken and

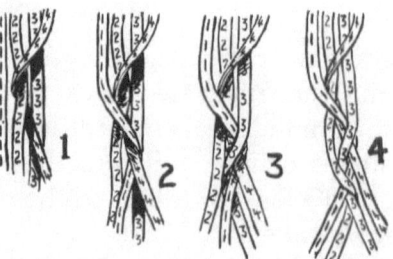

passed over strands 2 and 4, and turned and brought forward between 2 and 4.

3. Strand 3 (on the side first worked) is taken and passed over strands 1 and 4, and turned and brought forward between the two.

4. Strand 2 is taken, passed over strands 1 and 3, turned and then brought forward between 1 and 3.

5. This sequence is repeated.

Lariat plaiting must be kept "tight," that is, plaited close, and the flat strands must be turned as they twist round the two strands they have overlaid.

TO FOLD A FLAG FOR "BREAKING"

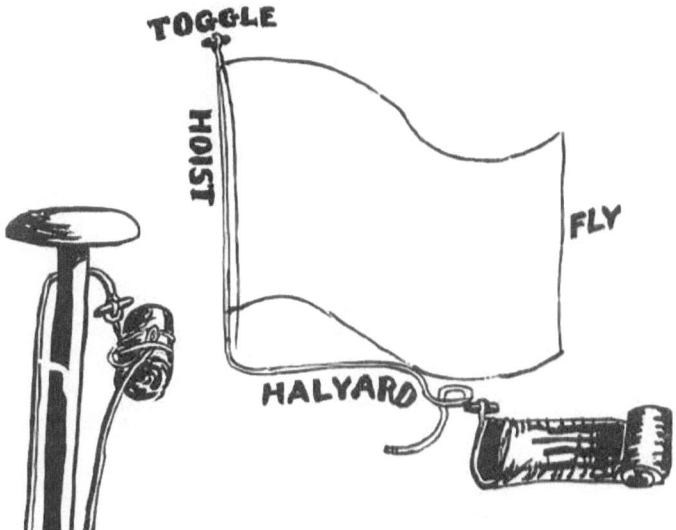

The flag is folded neatly along its length four to eight times, and then the fly is either folded, concertina fashion, or rolled towards the hoist. The toggle is uppermost on the hoist, and the halyard is on the lower side of the hoist.

The halyard is wrapped tightly round the flag, and then bent, and the loop pressed under the last rollings, held by the pressure of the cord against the bunting of the flag.

The toggle is fastened to the eye of the halyard on the mast, and the free end of the flag hoist is fastened to the other end of the mast halyard with a double sheet or crossover bend.